SO-CSX-297

Making Mountains

by Margot Shales • illustrated by Steve Gardner

Chapters

Harcourt

Orlando   Boston   Dallas   Chicago   San Diego

Visit *The Learning Site!*

www.harcourtschool.com

MOUNTAINS OF QUESTIONS

Stretching along the west coast of North America from southern Canada into northern California is a long range of mountains called the Cascades. The Cascade range has more than a dozen *volcanoes.*

Nearly all the volcanoes in the Cascades are either extinct (no longer active) or dormant (erupting only once in a great while). One of those dormant volcanoes, Mount St. Helens, woke up and erupted on March 27, 1980. In a remote part of Washington state, Mount St. Helens blasted columns of ash as high as 11,000 feet, dropping it on cities hundreds of miles away. The photograph on the cover of this book shows the Mount St. Helens eruption.

Another volcano, in Oregon, is called Crater Lake. This lake is actually a crater—a hollowed-out area around a volcano's opening—from a volcano that literally blew its top more than 6,000 years ago. Over time, the crater filled with water, creating the lake.

Mt. Baker
Glacier Peak
Mt. Ranier
Mt. St. Helens
Mt. Adams
Mt. Hood
Mt. Jefferson
Three Sisters
Newberry Caldera
Mt. Thielsen
Crater Lake
Mt. Mcloughlin
Mt. Shasta
Lassen Peak

Volcanic mountain ranges such as the Cascades once raised numerous questions for geologists, scientists who study Earth. For example: *What are volcanoes? Why are they often located in groups? Why do volcanoes and earthquakes often occur in the same areas?*

Of course, many other related questions also kept scientists scratching their heads for many centuries, including: *How are mountains formed? How do the fossils of sea animals get inside mountain rock—thousands of feet above the sea? Why do we find the same kinds of rocks and fossils on different continents, such as Africa and South America, that are separated by oceans?*

Areas of Earthquake Activity

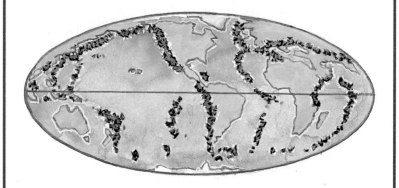

Dark gray shading indicates the danger areas.

Areas of Volcanic Activity

Dark gray shading indicates the danger areas.

As recently as a hundred years ago, geologists had no answers to these questions. Much of Earth was still a puzzle.

Once, the main theory about how mountains are formed was that the "skin" of Earth was shrinking. Have you ever seen how the skin of a rotting apple wrinkles up as its sides fall in, forming ridges and pits? Geologists thought that Earth was like that apple and that its crust—the "skin"—was shrinking. They supposed that this was because Earth was cooling down. A ridge was a mountain range, and a pit, or cavity, held an ocean or sea.

The "shrinking skin" theory seemed to answer a lot of questions. For instance, as Earth's skin wrinkled up, the theory said, the ocean drained away from high places such as mountains. Lots of sea animals were left without water and died on dry land. This explained why their fossils were found at the tops of mountains far from the sea.

The theory also suggested that the draining water, because of the shrinking skin, exposed land bridges between continents. Animals searching for edible material could have crossed these bridges in an ancient migration. This explained why fossils of the same animals were found on continents separated by an ocean.

Despite the fact that many scientists liked the "shrinking skin" theory, there were questions it didn't answer. For example, why did continents that were oceans apart contain the same kinds of rocks? Animals migrate in search of territory or nourishing food, but rocks do not.

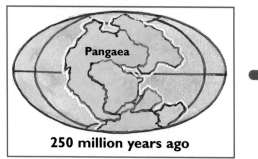

250 million years ago

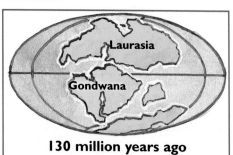

130 million years ago

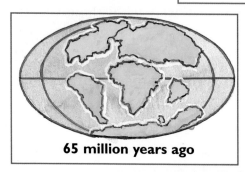

65 million years ago

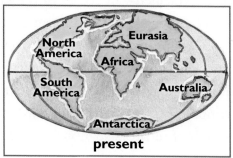

present

Finally, along came a man named Alfred Wegener (1880–1930), a German scientist with an idea that, in time, would explain everything. The only trouble was that few people believed him.

Alfred Wegener

Around the turn of the twentieth century, Wegener noticed an odd thing about the continents of South America and Africa. The coasts that faced each other across the Atlantic Ocean seem to fit together like pieces of a jigsaw puzzle. Even stranger, if he took the shapes of all the continents and cut them out like a puzzle, he could piece them *all* together. The fit wasn't perfect, but to Wegener it seemed too close to be mere coincidence.

Eduard Suess

Perhaps, Wegener thought, at one time all continents were one huge supercontinent. He called this continent *Pangaea,* which means "all land."

Wegener wasn't the first person to notice the snug fit of South America and Africa. The English scientist Francis Bacon

Francis Bacon

had been curious about it as early as 1620. Later, in the early 1900s, a geologist named Eduard Suess noted that all the southern continents shared the same rock formations. He suggested that these continents had all been part of a giant southern continent at one time; he named that ancient land mass *Gondwanaland.*

CATCH MY DRIFT?

Wegener was one of the first scientists to say that all the continents—not just the southern ones—had once been connected. What's more, he was the first with an idea about why this super-continent might have broken up into smaller continents.

Wegener believed the continents moved very slowly, maybe only an inch or two each year. One way to think about continents—and to understand Wegener's theory—is to compare the continents to enormous ice floes on an almost frozen sea. Over time, the tides in the ocean beneath broke the ice away from a polar ice cap. Each ice floe was carried in a different direction by the tide and the ocean.

Just as those huge cakes of ice were once part of a polar ice cap, the continents were once part of one landmass. Continents, Wegener said, were adrift on a foundation of moving rock—a lower level of Earth's crust. Yes, Wegener suggested, the continents and mountains do seem "hard as rock," but maybe the lower levels of Earth's crust aren't quite as solid as the surface.

He also theorized that some mountain ranges might have been created when continents crashed together. He suggested that India, once separate from the rest of Asia, moved north. Where it bumped into Asia, it produced the Himalayan mountain range. Furthermore, couldn't all mountains have been formed over time by continents crashing together? Wegener called his theory *continental drift.*

Though many people found Wegener's idea interesting, many more thought the "shrinking skin" theory made more sense. Some scientists pointed out that rock is too rigid and strong to be moved around as Wegener suggested. He could not prove, after all, that Earth's crust had a less-solid level far below the surface.

Wegener couldn't explain another puzzle either: What kind of force inside Earth could move continents around like ice floes on a northern sea? Wegener talked about "tides" in Earth's crust, but no one was convinced.

At a 1928 meeting of geologists, when Wegener presented his ideas, the most important geologists of the day attacked them. Because he couldn't answer all their questions, the geologists tore apart Wegener's theory until no one believed it could be true. Two years after this discouraging reception, Wegener died during a trip to Greenland. If he had lived another thirty years, he would have had proof that he was right.

The proof came with the study of mid-ocean ridges in the 1950s and 1960s. These ridges are actually underwater mountain ranges, many thousands of miles long. The mid-ocean ridges form a chain that circles the entire Earth.

While scientists had known about the mid-ocean ridges for years, in the 1960s they discovered something new. The sea floor on either side of these underwater mountain ranges is spreading—the two sides are moving away from each other. As the sea floor spreads apart, a volcano of sorts forms. Molten rock bubbles up from under the sea floor and fills the crack at the top of the mountain ridge. This molten rock, called *magma*, rapidly cools and helps rebuild the mountain range even as it is being pulled apart. This fiery mountain-making process never stops, widening the floor of the Atlantic Ocean by about an inch each year.

This discovery gave rise to a new theory, built upon Wegener's theory of continental drift. This new theory was called *plate tectonics*. According to this theory, Earth's crust is made up of giant "plates" that fit together like a jigsaw puzzle. There are six large plates and about twelve smaller ones, but the pieces of this puzzle are always moving and crashing into each other. Some move as fast as three and a half inches a year, while others creep along at less than half an inch a year. So Wegener was right: The continents do move, and there are forces deep underground that are slowly changing the face of the planet.

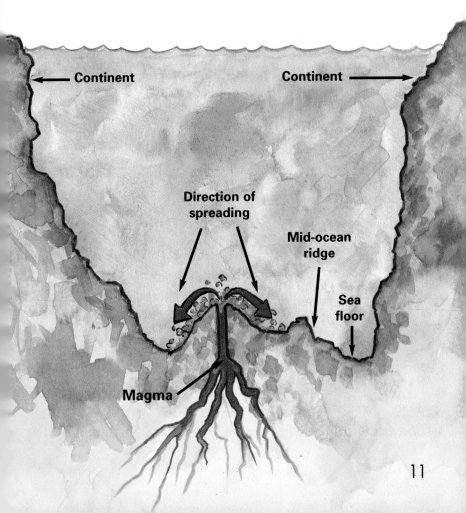

Continent

Continent

Direction of spreading

Mid-ocean ridge

Sea floor

Magma

WHEN PLATES COLLIDE

The movement of Earth's giant plates has made the world we see today. The plates break up continents and drag them to pieces. For example, the skinny finger of Baja California, which forms part of Mexico's Pacific coastline, exists because a plate is moving north. That plate tore some land away from the side of Mexico. The movement of plates also creates dry land. The continents themselves are sea floor

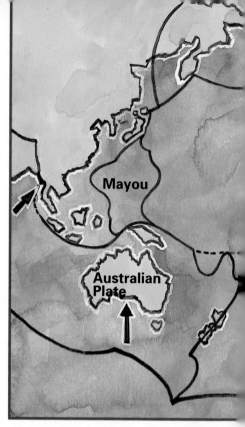

Tectonic Plate Movement

that has, over time, been pushed up out of the water by tectonic movement. That explains why people discover fossils of sea creatures so far from the sea. The plates even build mountains. The Alps in Europe, the Andes in South America, and even the Cascades are located where plates crash into each other, crumpling up land and raising giant peaks.

When two plates meet, one of three things can happen. They can move away from each other, as they do at the mid-ocean ridges. They can rub against each other, which

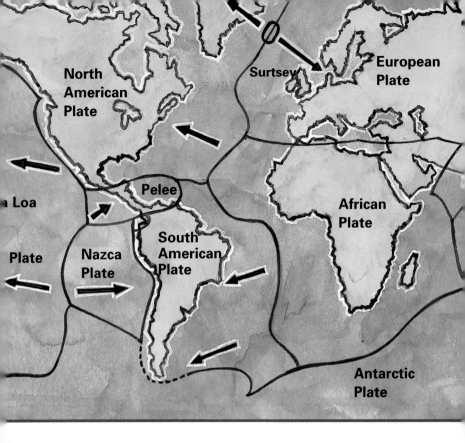

happens along some earthquake faults. The North American plate and the Pacific plate slide against each other along North America's west coast. Every time the plates slip, there is an earthquake—sometimes a violent one. Finally, two plates can push against each other. When this happens, one of the plates eventually is forced under the other. The plate that rides up high crumples and wrinkles and forms a mountain range. The plate that gets pushed down heats up and melts. Hot magma rises and forces its way out of Earth's crust. When the magma pours out—usually in a big explosion—a volcano is born.

13

Magma rises through volcano vent.

Ocean plate

Continental plate

Plate breaks up and becomes magma.

14

Why do volcanoes become dormant or extinct? That process, too, is the result of plate movement. Because the plates are always shifting, over time, a volcano actually moves away from the spot where it was born. The magma that used to feed the original volcano then begins to build a new volcano. The Hawaiian Islands were formed in this way. They are actually the tops of a range of volcanic mountains. If the mountains beneath the Hawaiian Islands sat on the dry land of a continent, they would be the tallest mountains on Earth.

As the plates move around, Earth's surface changes. What does the future hold in store? Some scientists have a hypothesis: In another 50 million years, they say, North and South America will split apart—and Africa will crowd in on the Mediterranean Sea. According to their theory, a piece of Africa will slide north into the Indian Ocean, and California will split off from the rest of North America—but it won't fall into the ocean (as people like to say). Instead, it will slide north and west on a collision course with Alaska. Of course, these predictions are only speculation.

Earth is always remaking itself. It takes billions of years, but sooner or later, the surface will become "new" again. When an earthquake occurs or when a volcano erupts, we are seeing plate tectonics in action. The noise and shaking are signs of Earth renewing itself.

AN EARTH-MOVING GLOSSARY

active volcanoes that are still producing ash and magma and that occasionally erupt

continental drift Wegener's theory that Earth once had one gigantic land mass that, over time, broke into the continents, which "drifted" into their current arrangement

crater a hollowed-out area around a volcano's opening

dormant volcanoes that are still active but rarely erupt

extinct volcanoes that no longer erupt

geologist a scientist who studies the earth and its history

lava magma that has found its way to Earth's surface

magma molten rock, found in mid-ocean ridges and volcanoes; called lava once it appears above ground

mid-ocean ridge an underwater mountain range where new sea floor forms

plate tectonics a theory that enormous pieces, or "plates," of Earth's crust are always moving

volcano a mountainous vent in Earth's crust that releases molten rock